DATE DUE

Robert Peary

and the Quest
for the North Pole

Explorers of New Worlds

Robert Peary

and the Quest
for the North Pole

Daniel E. Harmon

Chelsea House Publishers
Philadelphia

Prepared for Chelsea House Publishers by:
OTTN Publishing, Stockton, N.J.

CHELSEA HOUSE PUBLISHERS
Editor in Chief: Sally Cheney
Associate Editor in Chief: Kim Shinners
Production Manager: Pamela Loos
Art Director: Sara Davis
Director of Photography: Judy L. Hasday
Project Editors: LeeAnne Gelletly, Brian Baughan
Series Designer: Keith Trego

First Printing
1 3 5 7 9 8 6 4 2

Library of Congress Cataloging-in-Publication Data

Harmon, Daniel E.
   Robert Peary and the quest for the North Pole /
   Daniel E. Harmon.
     p. cm. – (Explorers of new worlds)
Includes bibliographical references and index (p.).
ISBN 0-7910-6440-9 (alk. paper)–ISBN 0-7910-6441-7
   (pbk. : alk. paper)
1. Peary, Robert E. (Robert Edwin), 1856–1920. 2.
Explorers–United States–Biography. 3. Arctic regions–
Discovery and exploration. 4. North Pole–Discovery
and exploration. I. Title. II. Series.

G635.P4 H28 2001
919.804–dc21
[B]   2001028204

Contents

Robert Peary, wearing Eskimo clothing and holding a harpoon, during one of his attempts to reach the North Pole. Peary spent much of his life dedicated to this quest.

Heartrending Failure in the Frozen North I

obert Peary looked around. In every direction he saw a frozen desert: flat ice, crude ridges of broken ice slabs, murky horizons where the polar ice field met the sky. Though his face was frozen, he was unaware of the cold. But on the inside he was in great pain, almost to the point of tears. Peary was gravely depressed—not by the bleakness and torturous cold of the far north, but by the realization that he had to leave it.

The year was 1906. Explorers from several countries were racing to the **Arctic Circle** to make one of the last great journeys in human history: the trek to the North

Pole. Peary believed in his heart that he could be first to reach the Pole. At this moment he was closer to it than any human ever had been; he was only 174 miles to the south. Yet he could not get closer. On the long sled journey northward from the base camp at Cape Hecla, blizzards had kept his party pinned down for days on end. Their carefully measured stores of food had dwindled while they waited for the weather to clear. Now they had reached the point of no return. There was–hopefully–just enough food remaining to get them to the base camp if they turned back immediately.

Bitterly, Peary decided they had to turn back. What would be the point of reaching the Pole if he did not live to tell about it?

There was little time to dwell on this failure, however. The men faced a very difficult challenge: getting home alive. The ship they had sailed on from New York, the *Roosevelt,* was more than 250 miles away. Some of their sled dogs had already died. The arctic wind was almost unbearable. The ice over which they traveled was often perilously thin. In one place, they crossed a weak surface for two miles, fearing that with each new step one of them might plunge into the unbearably cold Arctic

Ocean beneath. That would mean almost certain death, as the heavy fur clothing each man wore would drag him quickly down into the depths.

Finally, the white hills of Greenland came into view. Peary had aimed for the north coast of Greenland rather than the camp they had left at Cape Hecla. He knew the drifting ice pack was carrying them steadily to the east.

Near the coast, they met another party of explorers from the *Roosevelt.* These men were lost, starving, and near death. Peary's men were not doing much better, but at least they knew which way to go.

With their food supply gone, the exhausted explorers sighted some musk oxen. They were almost too weak to aim their guns and shoot the wild game. When they finally slew and butchered the animals, they ate the meat raw. They spent two days eating and resting, recovering their strength for the difficult trek the rest of the way to the *Roosevelt.*

Peary knew they could now make it back to the ship. But the *Roosevelt* and its crew would also be having a difficult time surviving the arctic harshness. Would the ship still be seaworthy? Would Peary and his men reach civilization–much less return another year to conquer the North Pole?

A Boy Bent on
Adventure

Large chunks of ice float in this bay on the coast of Greenland, dwarfing the small boat. From the age of six, when he read about the adventures of American explorer Elisha Kent Kane in Greenland, Robert Peary was interested in exploring the frozen north. He wasn't alarmed by the description of Kane's ship being crushed in ice; he was fascinated!

2

Robert Edwin Peary was born May 6, 1856, in Cres-son, Pennsylvania, but grew up on the Maine coast near Portland. His father, Charles Peary, died when Robert was not yet three years old.

Robert, called "Bert" by his family, loved books. He also loved the outdoors, and grew up roaming the forests. Young Robert was an excellent student. After his first few years in school, Robert was sent to boarding schools so he could advance more quickly in his studies. He liked math and writing, but his passion was nature. He became an avid bird-watcher and could identify most of the feathered creatures he encountered.

Peary had a slight speech disorder. It embarrassed him, but he believed he could overcome it. With long, hard practice, he eventually did. He became such a fine public speaker that he spoke at his high school graduation. For his topic, he chose the mysteries of nature.

Peary earned a scholarship to Bowdoin College in Brunswick, Maine, where he studied engineering. He was highly respected by his professors for his knowledge and intelligence. Peary also was an energetic athlete. The tall, broad-shouldered teen was a fine sailor, swimmer, and rower. He could hurl a baseball farther than any of his classmates. He loved to walk, often trekking 25 or 30 miles a day.

Peary graduated from Bowdoin with honors. After college, he went to work as a surveyor in Fryeburg, Maine. Surveying was only one of his talents and interests. Peary could draw, he loved to ice skate, and he acted in local plays. He was also a skilled taxidermist—a craftsperson who stuffs dead birds and animals for display—and he made good money for his taxidermy services. He even became known for his ability to tame wild horses.

Peary was obviously enjoying himself—but he wanted to see much more of the world. He went to Washington, D.C., and took a job as a **draftsman** for the U.S. Coast and Geodetic Survey. Then he took a test to join the Civil Engineer Corps, a special service within the U.S. Navy. The examination was very hard. Few passed it . . . but Peary did, and he was accepted into the Civil Engineer Corps.

Peary first worked in Key West, Florida. Then, in 1884 he was sent to Central America. A team of engineers was looking for a suitable place to construct a canal between the Atlantic and Pacific oceans. Peary's team of engineers explored Nicaragua, looking for a potential canal site.

In the jungle, Peary had his share of adventure. The trees, vines, and plants were so dense that the party of engineers sometimes had to measure their progress in yards rather than miles. They climbed into the trees to scout ahead for the best course. They sloshed through dark, stagnant, scary waters.

Little wonder that after Nicaragua, Peary was ready for a change. He turned his attention in the opposite direction—to Greenland and the far north.

The adventurer Elisha Kent Kane (1820-1857) was one of the first Americans to explore the Arctic Circle. The route he helped pioneer to the North Pole would eventually become known to explorers as the "American Way."

For years, Peary had been curious about the frozen Arctic. Two of his heroes were Elisha Kent Kane and Charles Francis Hall. In separate expeditions, these men had joined international efforts to rescue the lost crew of Sir John Franklin—or at least to find their remains and learn what had happened. Sir John Franklin and his crew had left England in June 1845 to search for a **Northwest Passage**. They never returned. Neither Kane nor Hall had succeeded in solving the Franklin mystery, but both had contributed to the growing body of knowledge about the Arctic region.

Kane had sailed northward along the Greenland coast in 1853. He had learned to cope with the harsh northern climate by living and traveling as the Eskimos did. He set important examples that later Arctic explorers, including Peary, would follow.

In 1871, Hall had gone by ship almost as far north as the Englishman Edward Parry had gone in 1827. He, like so many voyagers in the bleak northern ocean, had been stopped by ocean currents and fierce blizzards.

Kane and Hall had mapped out a route toward the North Pole. This plan involved sailing north through the Davis Strait and Baffin Bay between Greenland and Canada, then continuing through Smith Sound into Kane Basin and beyond, to the edge of the Arctic ice pack. From there, travel would have to proceed over the ice via dog ***sledge***.

Peary longed to make his own mark as a finder of new places. In his diary, he mused about the awesome feeling that must have come over earlier explorers as their eyes gazed on new lands. He wanted to experience that feeling. But the only major conquests remaining in the 1880s were the most difficult: the North and South Poles. He was not ready to attempt an assault on the North Pole. But he was eager to begin learning about the Arctic frontier.

First Forays into the Icy Wilderness

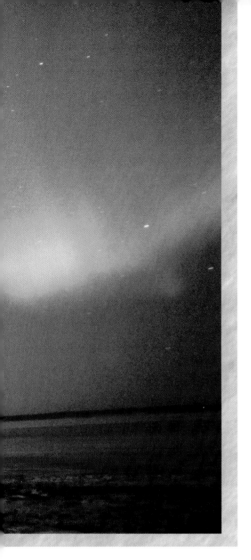

The colorful "northern lights," or aurora borealis, are among the wonders of the frozen north. In 1886, Robert Peary set out on his first Arctic exploration.

3

The year was 1886. With a Danish friend named Christian Maigaard, Peary set out to do something no one ever had done before: cross the vast, snow-encrusted island of Greenland from west to east. Peary wanted to see what the frigid Arctic region was like. This expedition would give him a taste of it.

The dangers and difficulties here turned out to be no milder than those of Nicaragua—but very different. Instead of snakes, mosquitoes, muddy mires, jungle flies, and stifling heat, he confronted endless ice, with unexpected hazards. Deep cuts in the snow called *crevasses* could swallow a person. In fact, the pair of intrepid trekkers fell into crevasses, but managed to escape. Peary also skidded into an icy river, but again managed to save himself.

It was all too much for them. After struggling for about 100 miles, they gave up and returned home.

The next year, the government sent Peary back to Central America. Once again, he was told to look for a possible site to build a crossing between the oceans. (This canal would eventually be built across Panama during the early part of the 20th century.) This was important work, but Peary's heart was no longer in the tropics. After almost a year, he returned to Washington, D.C. From then on, he would focus on exploring the frozen Arctic.

First, though, young Robert had a more important matter at hand. He was in love. He married Josephine Diebitsch in August 1888; their wedding took place in America's capital city.

At this point in history, the great island of Greenland had not been completely explored. In fact, Europeans didn't know it was an island. Peary and other explorers suspected it might extend as far north as the top of the world. They soon would learn this belief was wrong. In 1891, Peary set out with a party of scientists to investigate the unknown parts of Greenland. Josephine went with them. The expedition had the financial backing of several scientific societies. The young man was looking forward to exploring the region of the awesome, colorful ***aurora borealis***, or "northern lights."

The mission had a disastrous beginning. One day, after their ship *Kite* had entered ice-jammed waters, the vessel's ***tiller*** was thrown wildly to one side when ice rammed the rudder. The tiller broke Peary's leg. He spent weeks healing in a crude cast before he could travel with the dog sledges.

After setting up a base camp on the northwestern coast of Greenland, Peary and one companion, Eivind Astrup, set out across the snowy expanse to the east and north. They traveled in subzero temperatures for hundreds of miles. The men had a team of 20 dogs to pull their sledges, which were loaded with supplies. Dog sledges in Peary's time were made of sturdy wooden frames with steel runners. They could carry more than 600 pounds of provisions–most of it food for the dog teams.

Crossing a high ridge, Peary and Astrup came upon a valley where the snow had partly melted. Here the weather was warm compared to the icy plains. Wild oxen lived in the valley–welcome meat for the men and their dogs. Across the plateau on the other side of the valley they discovered a large bay of the ocean. The date was July 4th, so Peary named it Independence Bay. The land north of the bay was different from other parts of Greenland. Peary was excited to find wildflowers, bumblebees, and more oxen. The temperature, amazingly, was 70 degrees.

Peary and Astrup now realized that Greenland was an island, hemmed in by the Arctic Ocean to the north. It was time to return to base camp. The return journey was not nearly as pleasant. They again had to endure the hardships of traveling over snow and ice. At one point, a blizzard kept them pinned down for two and a half days. When they finally reached the main camp, they had traveled more than a thousand miles. Their fellow scientists at the camp were very impressed. Already, Robert Peary had earned respect as an Arctic explorer.

Two years later, Peary and his wife were back in Greenland for further exploration. This trip was to

Robert Peary with his wife, Josephine. The couple was married in August 1888; their first child was born in September 1893—in the Arctic.

become a family affair. Josephine Peary brought a nurse with her, for she was expecting a baby. Marie Ahnighito Peary was born in the Arctic on September 12, 1893.

Peary's decision to take his wife on these two adventures was unusual. Sea captains sometimes took their wives and children on their voyages. But a hazardous journey into an isolated, unknown region was a very different situation.

Josephine was up to the challenge. She was able to help around the base camp, and after returning home she lectured and raised money to help support her husband's explorations.

The birth of their daughter was one of the few happy moments of the 1893-95 expedition. Peary

Peary's Right-Hand Man

Matthew Henson and Robert Peary met in 1887 at the Washington, D.C., hat maker's shop where Henson worked. Peary needed an assistant for his surveying travels. Henson wanted to see the world, a dream few black Americans could achieve in the 1800s. It was an ideal match.

Henson would come to know the Arctic just as well as Peary. Henson was put in charge of taking care of the dogs and sledges. He also saved the day more than once with his great hunting skills, and his friendship with the Eskimos was often useful. The Inuits greatly respected him for his strength, courage, hunting prowess, and ability to get the utmost from his dog teams.

unfortunately got no farther into the snowy island than he had before.

Peary was traveling by sledge with two other men: a hardy African American named Matthew Henson, who had been Peary's engineering assistant since his final year in Central America, and another explorer named Hugh Lee. While exploring Greenland this time, Peary's party had trouble with the dogs, a sledge was wrecked and had to be repaired, and Lee became desperately sick and could not walk. Lee told his companions to return to camp alone. The leader would not hear of it. "We will all get home," Peary insisted, "or none of us will." He personally nursed Lee back to health. By the time the three men made it back to their base, only one of their dogs was still alive.

The ordeal had taken its toll on Peary. According to his friends, he seemed in a daze at times on the desolate ice. He didn't appear to know where he was or to care whether he made it back to civilization. But although Peary viewed the expedition as a failure, fellow scientists were beginning to regard him as the most capable man exploring the Arctic.

This painting shows Peary preparing to disembark from his ship; his dog teams are straining to get started for the Pole. However, Peary would first endure many disappointing years as he attempted to reach his goal.

Four Years of Frustration 4

In 1898, Peary again took leave from his navy job to explore the north. He was given permission to live and work in the region for as long as five years. He was finally ready to tackle the ultimate goal: the North Pole.

Peary knew there was but one way to reach the Pole. He would have to go as far north as possible by ship, then strike out over the ice-covered Arctic Ocean with dog sledges. Dog teams could travel as far as 70 miles a day if the weather was good and the ice smooth and solid.

The Arctic *ice cap* is a mass of *floes*, floating ice islands many yards thick and sometimes as wide as the eye can see. Humans and dog sledges can live and travel on the ice without breaking through. It is not a solid, connected ice pack, though. It shifts and changes with the seasons and the ocean currents.

Sometimes the floes are packed tightly together, and travelers can move from one right onto the next. At other places, the ice is divided by areas of open water called *leads*. Travelers have to go around the leads or wait and hope the currents will close them up.

Naturally, Peary found ice travel to be very dangerous. The moving ice pack would crack. Great sheets of ice would crash against and slide over one another, rumbling loudly and shaking everything nearby. At other places, the ice would separate into leads. Peary's men encountered one lead more than two miles wide.

Peary had developed his strategy for conquering the Pole many years earlier, before he ever saw the Arctic. After reading the details of other explorers' failed attempts, he decided a team of only a few men—mostly Eskimos—traveling by dog sled would have the best chance. A large party would depart the base camp. At points along the trail, some would turn back to the base, leaving the food they had

This aerial view of a portion of the polar ice cap shows how ice floes are jammed together. The areas of open water are called leads. Peary and his men had to be cautious not to break through the ice.

hauled for those who would continue. That way the few who remained for the final dash would have ample supplies for the return trip.

An English nobleman, Alfred Harmsworth, gave Peary an old steamship named the *Windward.* Peary's expedition proceeded into the icy North

The people Peary found living in the far north were the Eskimos, or Inuits. Some of the Inuits live within several hundred miles of the Pole. They are rugged individuals, able to bear severe cold and weather conditions that most people could hardly endure. The Inuits fish and hunt wild animals.

Atlantic, but the *Windward* was blocked by ice floes off Ellesmere Island, west of Greenland. The explorers made their winter camp near the center of Ellesmere Island. It was always dark. In the Arctic, the sun stays below the horizon both night and day in winter. And it is very cold—far below zero—and windy.

Despite the numbing weather, Peary, Henson, Dr. T. S. Dedrick, and some Eskimos set out by dog sledge from their camp. Peary believed he could travel over the frozen sea and reach an abandoned outpost called Fort Conger. It was just a small hut that had been built by an American expedition under Major Adolphus Greely in 1881. Fort Conger was 250 miles to the north, in the section of Ellesmere Island called Grant Land. From there, Peary would trek toward the Pole. Some of Peary's friends thought he was foolish to travel in wintertime, but Peary was not afraid.

He was amazed at the great ***monoliths*** of ice he encountered. Huge chunks of slowly moving ice under terrific pressure were pushed upward as high as 80 or 90 feet.

By the time they reached Fort Conger, the men and dogs were exhausted. Some of their equipment was damaged. They had expected to find food stored at the outpost by previous explorers, but there was little that was fit to eat.

Physically, Peary was in a very bad way. His feet had frozen during the journey, and he could not stand. The pain was almost unbearable. Henson, Dedrick, and the Eskimos bundled him in furs on a bunk inside a cold hut and scrounged in the darkness for food.

They remained there six weeks. Because of Peary's condition and their low food supply, there was no way they could go farther into the bleak void. At last his companions tied Peary atop a dog sledge and took him back to the ship.

The journey over the ice had cost Peary dearly. Some of his toes, brittle with frostbite, had literally broken off his feet at Fort Conger. Because they had frozen, they became poisoned and rotting with a condition called ***gangrene***. This is a very dangerous affliction, in which areas of the body begin to decay due to a lack of blood flow. If the gangrene was not treated in time, the poison could have spread through Peary's whole body and killed him.

His remaining toes were later removed by surgeons. For the rest of his life, Peary would be forced to walk with an awkward, painful shuffle. But incredibly, within two months of returning to the ship, he resumed his explorations of Ellesmere Island. He still could not walk, so Peary demanded to be strapped to a sledge.

This time, rather than pressing northward again, Peary and his faithful Eskimo crew went west. They slowly made their way to the ice-capped top of Ellesmere Island—almost 5,000 feet above sea level.

During the summer and autumn of 1899, Peary gradually and painfully taught himself to walk again. He led supply trips to Fort Conger, storing food and *dry goods* there for a future attempt to reach the North Pole.

At the beginning of the new year, with his trusted companion Matthew Henson and a party of Eskimos, he set off to explore the uncharted northern region of Greenland. Blizzards sometimes forced them to stop and build *igloos* for shelter.

Because building materials such as timber are unavailable in the frozen north, the Inuits make huts from ice blocks—igloos—for shelter and storage.

Their way was made perilous by cracks and thin places on the surface. After all, they were driving their heavy sledges over ice-covered water. At times, the dogs and sledges broke through the ice and fell into the frigid water! The men had to slosh through icy pools that sometimes were neck deep. In other places, they had to go over or around ridges of ice as high as 50 feet.

The adventurers reached the upper tip of Greenland—the northernmost piece of land on the planet. Then they went out over the frozen polar sea for several days until they ran out of solid ice beneath their feet.

Peary stayed in the north for two more years. At one point his wife and daughter came for a visit on the ship that brought supplies. After they left, Peary's crew sledged more provisions northward for his next dash toward the Pole.

Peary, Henson, and four Eskimos started onto the frozen polar ocean in spring 1902. They made it farther north than anyone had before, about 400 miles from their elusive destination. However, the ice pack was beginning to break up with the warming season. Great stretches of open water made it impossible for them to proceed. They had to turn back or risk being stranded in the icy ocean.

Although he still had not even come close to the North Pole, Peary had contributed much to science by exploring the northern coast of Greenland and Ellesmere Island. He considered his five-year expedition to be a failure, however. "My dream of sixteen years," he wrote, "is ended." At that moment in his life, Peary believed it was impossible for anyone to reach the North Pole.

He soon would change his mind.

Peary on the deck of his ship, the Roosevelt. *The vessel was built specifically for exploring in icy northern waters.*

A Very Special Ship 5

T hose four years of seeming failure in the Arctic convinced Peary that a special ship was needed to sail far enough north for a successful polar dash. It must have an unusually strong hull that could withstand a battering from tons of hard ice. It would be squeezed as great sections of ice under pressure pushed against it from all sides. The ship would have to be designed to rise to the surface of the enclosing ice, last through the winter thus stranded, and still be seaworthy when the ice pack loosened and set it free the following spring.

No ship ever had been built for such a strange and

Robert Peary's ship Roosevelt, *named for then-president Theodore Roosevelt (inset), was built to withstand the strain of a polar voyage through thick ice.*

hazardous purpose. One would have to be specially made. How could Peary afford to build any vessel at all, much less one crafted and equipped for voyages into ice?

Fortunately for Peary, his work had attracted the interest of some wealthy people and powerful organizations interested in science and exploration.

They formed the Peary Arctic Club and donated about half the money for his ice-breaking ship. Peary raised the rest himself by writing books and giving lectures on what the frozen north was like.

Thus was built the *Roosevelt*, a sturdy, 184-foot-long vessel with both sail and steam power. The bow, reinforced with metal, had a very sharp slant so it could be driven onto obstructing ice. Then the ship would use its weight to break through. The vessel was named after President Theodore Roosevelt, an avid outdoorsman and explorer. Its captain was Bob Bartlett, a wise Canadian seafarer who knew much about the ice floes of the far North Atlantic.

Peary had been promoted to the rank of commander by the Navy Department. He knew he would never be happy as a navy engineering officer, though. He was an explorer.

The *Roosevelt* was ready to depart New York in July 1905, three years after Peary's return from Ellesmere Island. Peary intended to plunge headlong into the Arctic Ocean and try for the Pole that year.

On the way up the coast of Greenland, he hired a group of hardy Eskimo men, who brought along their families and dog teams. They packed aboard enough raw fish, walrus, and whale meat to last them for a long time.

Ocean voyages aboard work ships were usually smelly affairs. Aboard the *Roosevelt*, the odors from the meat supply, dogs, and Eskimos—who typically did not bathe—were almost overpowering to the Americans. But Peary had already made many personal sacrifices in his quest to reach the North Pole. He was ready to endure shipboard life without complaint.

The voyage was easy as far north as Inglefield Gulf on the Greenland coast. Then the *Roosevelt* had to prove its worth. Bartlett nosed the ship into the thickening ice.

It was a fine icebreaker, forging a crude path across the white surface of the sea. At places, the ice was higher than the ship's main deck. The vessel was jolted and bruised repeatedly. Its rudder was badly damaged.

Finally, Bartlett maneuvered the ship into an expanse of fairly open ocean where the ice floes were looser, making progress easier. The ocean currents were treacherous, though, sweeping masses and chunks of ice rapidly southward between Grant Land and Greenland. This caused unexpected, violent collisions between ship and ice.

Peary and Bartlett, besides being leaders of the expedition, showed the crew they were capable sailors as well. They sometimes climbed the rigging to serve as lookouts, directing the *Roosevelt* through the ice.

After a grueling battle with the floes, the *Roosevelt* reached the north shore of Ellesmere Island at Cape Sheridan. Then the surging floes heaved the ship upward. It settled atop the ice. It would stay there through the coming winter while Peary set out for the Pole.

The men took some of the food and supplies off the ship and stored them on the icy island. This was a security measure, ensuring that they would have something to live on if the shifting ice pack sank or severely damaged the ship.

The explorers soon faced a problem almost as serious as damage to the *Roosevelt*: tons of the whale meat they had brought with them had spoiled. Eighty of their 200 dogs died after eating the bad food. It had to be thrown away.

The men now had to rely on their hunting skills for meat. They were able to shoot a number of large musk oxen, caribou, and Arctic hares.

The food that Arctic explorers had to eat was not exactly appetizing. Peary lost about 30 pounds on one trip. After enduring dried and frozen meat for months on end, Captain Bartlett confessed to overeating when he returned to civilization. "I sneaked off every time I could and ordered a big thick steak piled up with fine greasy fried onions," he later wrote.

Besides hunting, there was much other work to do. For example, the crew made a form of condensed food called *pemmican* by grinding up meat, blending it with fat, and shaping it into cakes. Peary and his sledge team would carry pemmican because it was lightweight and easy to transport.

Meanwhile, they built sledges and made winter clothing from the furs and skins of bears, foxes, and seals. Peary had learned these and other Arctic survival skills from his Eskimo friends.

He decided to haul provisions west to Cape Hecla. There he would set up a base camp for his trek to the North Pole over the ice sea.

Peary's party set out for the Pole in mid-February 1906. Matthew Henson led the way in lightweight, rapid sledges. His job was to find the safest path through the cracked ice; the others would follow his tracks. By the time they caught up with him at the end of each stage of the journey, Henson had built an igloo to shelter the men and dogs from piercing winds and temperatures that dropped to 50 degrees below zero.

Snowstorms occurred frequently. One blizzard kept Peary's expedition pinned inside their igloos for almost a week. Finally, Peary and seven men were able to press northward once more. However, they were running low on supplies, and a wide gap in the ice behind them prevented other members of

Eskimo fur leggings, from the Field Museum of Natural History in Chicago. Although some polar explorers refused to adopt native dress and customs, the most successful, like Robert Peary and Roald Amundsen (the first man to reach the South Pole), used Inuit clothing and methods to help them reach their own goals.

the expedition from bringing up food. The members of Peary's little band went as far as they dared, leaving themselves barely enough food for the return trip to base camp. By April, they were hungry, half-frozen, and bone weary. More of their dogs had died.

The expedition was forced to turn back. Peary made the bitter calculation: they were only 174 miles from the Pole. Peary later reported that having to turn back after coming so close "gave me the deepest fit of the blues."

After the group reached Greenland, Peary successfully guided the expedition back to the *Roosevelt.* He then made a trip to the west, exploring new lands for about two months. Then it was time to sail home to New York—if that was possible.

The *Roosevelt* was in trouble. It had been seriously damaged by tons of shifting, crushing ice. The ice had knocked a large hole in the bottom of the ship. After the men patched it, more ice blocks knocked out the

When the men camped on the first night of the return journey, Peary's eyes hurt unbearably from exposure to the blinding, blowing snow. Ironically, he had to place snow packs on them to make the pain subside.

patch. They repaired it again.

By late 1906, the explorers had inched their way through the thickening ice pack down to Etah on the west coast of Greenland. There, they hauled the ailing vessel onshore. The hull and steering gear, they saw, had been damaged much worse than they had thought. Captain Bartlett doubted they could make the ship seaworthy. But they had to try, Peary urged him. Amazingly, on the bleak Greenland coast they were able to repair the *Roosevelt* well enough to put to sea.

They weren't safe yet, though. They ran aground farther down the Greenland coast and redamaged their flimsy propeller. Some of the crew had to get into the frigid water to fix it. Later, they ran into a fierce storm. Sea water poured into the ship's hold, and the men had to work feverishly to keep it pumped out.

Other storms hit them as they worked their way down the Canadian coast. Again they lost their rudder and had to rig a temporary replacement. At last, on Christmas Eve 1906, the *Roosevelt* reached New York. Peary was already planning his next—and last—attempt to reach the North Pole.

This illustration is based on a picture Robert Peary took of his men at the North Pole. From left to right are Ooqueah, holding the Navy League flag; Ootah, holding the banner of Peary's college fraternity; Matthew Henson, holding the polar flag; Egingwah, holding the Daughters of the American Revolution peace flag; and Seegloo, holding the Red Cross flag.

One Last Try 6

By the time the *Roosevelt* was ready to steam once more, Peary was more than 50 years old. For an explorer, he was an old man. He knew he would be able to make just one more attempt to reach the North Pole.

President Theodore Roosevelt himself inspected the restored ship that bore his name. He encouraged Peary, saying, "I believe in you."

The *Roosevelt* set forth on July 6, 1908. Once more, Peary carried as many Eskimos, dogs, foodstuffs, and other supplies as the ship could hold. The dog food alone—walrus and whale meat—weighed more than 100 tons.

Captain Bartlett later reported being repulsed by "the frightful noise, the choking stench and the terrible confusion" aboard the ship. He was relieved when they reached Cape Sheridan and began setting up base camp.

Peary then moved some supplies to a point on the shore west of Cape Sheridan called Cape Columbia. He had learned that the ice pack moved gradually eastward. By beginning his dash for the Pole farther west, he would make the ocean current work with him, not against him.

He made another important improvement in his strategy. This time, he sent a number of sledge teams northward to find the best path through the ice and take supplies as far as possible. They were to clear a trail through the broken ice ridges with shovels and other tools. Then Peary and a small party would make the final run to the Pole.

It was the end of February 1909 when the first dog sleds set out from Cape Columbia. The supply teams got Peary to within 140 miles of the Pole. Then, on April 2, he set out for the North Pole with Matthew Henson, four Eskimo helpers–Ooqueah, Ootah, Egingwah, and Seegloo–and 40 of the best sled dogs.

The drive north was not easy. Stinging, wind-blown ice and frustrating leads confronted them. Captain Bartlett later described their ordeal as "a month of terrible labor."

But then the weather improved. The men and the dogs were healthy. The ice conditions were as good as they ever were likely to be. Peary knew this would be his best chance to reach the North Pole.

Thanks to wise planning and fair weather, the final leg of the epic mission seemed almost easy. After four days, on April 6, Peary could tell by his compass and sextant readings that they were very near the Pole. But they were almost totally exhausted, so they stopped to sleep for a few hours.

Soon they awoke and pressed on. Henson and two of the Eskimos, Ootah and Seegloo, led the way, forging a trail through the last stretch of ice.

Actually, the party apparently went a little beyond the Pole. Peary's compass showed they were going southward down the other side of the world! It was a weird realization. Strangely, Peary did not feel jubilant. He fell into a dark mood and hardly spoke to his companions.

It was about 10 o'clock in the morning. To leave no doubt that they had crossed the Pole, Peary went some distance in different directions. He carefully recorded the various instrument readings.

"The Pole at last!!!" he wrote in his diary. "The prize of three centuries, my dream and ambition for twenty-three years. Mine at last. I cannot bring myself to realize it."

The weary explorers spent more than a day at the North Pole. Peary wrote a report of their feat and left it in a bottle. He photographed Henson and the Eskimos. They raised the United States flag and other pennants, and Peary wrote a note to Josephine.

Although they encountered tricky leads in the ice, their return to base was rather uneventful. It took them only two weeks to reach Cape Columbia. The Eskimos could hardly believe they had made it back to land so easily. "The devil is asleep or having trouble with his wife," joked one of them.

They built a monument of crude stones called a *cairn* at Cape Columbia. A wooden sign recorded the date they'd reached the North Pole. Peary knew no marker would last on the Arctic ice. He was certain the things they'd left at the Pole were already shifting. A permanent memorial could only be erected on solid ground.

This New York Times *front page heralds Peary's success in reaching the North Pole.*

Soon afterward, the triumphant explorers arrived at the *Roosevelt*. Terrible news awaited them. Ross Marvin, one of the dog team leaders, was dead. Many years later, Peary learned he had

Peary was frustrated to find that he could not announce his incredible accomplishment to the world right away. When he returned to the *Roosevelt*, he found the ship stuck in ice. The explorers had to wait for the summer thaw before they could begin the voyage to New York.

been killed by one of the Eskimos during a quarrel.

As the *Roosevelt* sailed home for New York, the ship stopped at Indian Harbor on the Labrador coast of Canada. There, the crew began to feel they were back in civilization after their year in the Arctic. There was a telegraph office at Indian Harbor. Peary was able to send messages to New York, letting the world know that the North Pole had finally been conquered.

"Have made good at last. I have the old Pole," he telegraphed to his wife.

"All well. Best love. God bless you. Hurry home," Josephine wired back.

But when he arrived in New York, Peary received the shock of his life. Another explorer, Dr. Frederick A. Cook, claimed to have reached the North Pole before Peary! Cook had been the doctor on Peary's 1891 expedition into Greenland. Since then, he had been exploring on his own. He stated that in April 1908–almost a year before Peary's achievement–he had reached the North Pole via a different, longer route.

Cook said he had sledged north from a point west of Peary's Cape Columbia base. After reaching the Pole, Cook reported, he had not returned to Ellesmere Island or Greenland. Instead, he traveled far to the east, arriving at last in Scandinavia. He was already a celebrated hero there. The Royal Geographical Society of Denmark and some Danish scholars had accepted Cook's claim.

Dr. Frederick A. Cook had been a member of a previous Peary expedition; in 1909 he claimed to have reached the North Pole before Peary and Henson.

Peary and Cook both received enthusiastic greetings from an excited American public. The North Pole had been mastered–and mastered by Americans! But everyone was puzzled. Had Cook really reached the Pole first? For that matter, had either man truly reached the North Pole? How could anyone be certain?

Peary was very angry. He was stunned to learn that he might not have been the first explorer to reach the Pole. He suspected Cook had lied in an attempt to receive credit that rightfully belonged to Peary. After talking with the Eskimos who had been with Cook in 1908, Peary became convinced Cook had never left sight of land or gone within several hundred miles of the North Pole.

Scientists soon began to doubt Cook as well. He apparently had kept no records on his expedition that would prove he had gone where he said he went. When his report of his journey was published, it contained many mistakes. With suspicion growing, Cook could not defend his claims effectively.

The public eventually realized that Cook was probably a fraud. Might Peary also be lying?

Many scientists believed Peary could not have traveled across the ice pack as rapidly as he said he had. Some said there were shadows in Peary's polar photographs that could not have appeared in those positions at that time of year if the pictures had actually been taken at the Pole.

The National Geographic Society in Washington, D.C., thoroughly examined Peary's notes and calculations. In the end, it determined that Peary had in fact reached the North Pole on April 6, 1909. Congress passed an official endorsement of his claim. The U.S. Navy promoted him to the rank of rear admiral.

Foreign scientists agreed. Among other awards, Peary was given the French Legion of Honor, the British Royal Geographic Society's Gold Medal, and honorary degrees from several European universities.

N° 446
16 Octobre 1909
50 Centimes

RÉDACTION
ET ADMINISTRATION
62, Rue de Provence,
PARIS
Téléphone.: 263-74

L'Assiette au Beurre

Le Pôle Nord

par

Leal da Camara

The Peary-Cook debate attracted worldwide interest, as can be seen in this French magazine cover from 1909. Although Cook was eventually proven to be a fraud, Peary's own claims have been questioned over the years.

The Long Quest for Recognition

7

espite Peary's endorsements, some scientists and historians still refused to accept Peary's claim. They debated it, in fact, long after his death.

Peary's descendants kept his diary and other records private until the 1980s. At the request of the National Geographic Society, the documents were examined by author Wally Herbert, a veteran polar explorer. In his 1989 book *The Noose of Laurels*, Herbert concluded Peary was off course on his final dash for the Pole and probably never arrived there. Herbert suspected Peary realized this and may have lived his final years in secret disappointment and shame.

The National Geographic Society then asked a respected organization called the Navigation Foundation to make a thorough study of all the records, including the diary. In January 1990, *National Geographic* magazine published the results of its study.

The Navigation Foundation supported Peary's claim. It concluded that Peary, Henson, and the four Eskimos—Ootah, Egingwah, Seegloo, and Ooqueah—had indeed arrived in the "near vicinity" (within five miles) of the North Pole. As far as scientific instruments of the period could determine in 1909, Peary had "realized his lifelong goal."

Gilbert Grosvenor, president of the National Geographic Society, wrote in an editorial that he believed the Navigation Foundation study finally awarded "due justice to a great explorer."

Like other explorers, Peary had his faults. His constant focus on conquering the North Pole kept him away from his family for years at a time. Many critics believe this demonstrated a selfish attitude. In her letters to him, Josephine sometimes sadly suggested that life was slipping away from them. It clearly was a very stressful marriage for her.

It was hard on their daughter, too. When she was nine, Marie wrote her dad in desperation: "I have been looking at your pictures it seems ten years and I am sick of looking at them. I want to see my father. I don't want people to think me an orphan."

Peary was also criticized for his treatment of the Inuits. Although he respected them for their ability to live in the harsh arctic climate, he did not consider them equals. He thought of them as laborers necessary to help him succeed. In addition, Peary thoughtlessly dug up several Eskimo graves in Greenland and sold the bones to a New York museum to raise money.

Another unappealing personal trait was a jealousy that sometimes drove him to anger. In a way, he seemed to believe he owned the North Pole and had won the right to be its first visitor. He didn't like it when other explorers used what he considered "his" routes through the ice. At the end of each expedition, he made his companions give him their diaries. They had to promise not to write books or give speeches about their travels. Peary wanted all the income from writing and lecturing for himself.

Peary's reasoning was partly understandable. He was, after all, the mastermind and organizer of the expeditions. He depended on lecturing and writing to help raise funds. Interestingly, though, Peary approved a book written by Henson, his longtime right-hand man. He even spent money to help promote Henson's book.

Peary died in 1920 at his home on Eagle Island, off Maine's rocky coast. He is buried among the nation's military heroes at Arlington National Cemetery in Washington, D.C.

In a way, it seems Robert Peary was born to conquer the Pole. He loved the far north and reveled in its hardships. He once wrote that whenever he was back in civilization, he yearned for "the great white desolation, the battles with the ice and the gales, the long, long, long Arctic night, the long, long, long Arctic day, the handful of odd but faithful Eskimos who had been my friends for years, the silence and the vastness of the great, white lovely North."

Today, there is still glory to be won by visiting the North Pole. Ever since the time of Peary, adventurers have sought to be "first" to the Pole–first to arrive by airship, first by airplane, first by icebreaker, first by snowmobile, even first by snow skis. The USS *Nautilus* in 1958 became the first submarine to cross the North Pole *beneath* the ice.

None of these latter-day conquerors, though, endured years of trials like Peary, using only the

A letter written by Peary during one of his attempts on the Pole. Peary is an example of persistence: despite seven failed attempts, he finally reached his goal.

tools and knowledge available in 1909. He alone earned the greatest Arctic honor: first human to lead an expedition to the North Pole.

When they reached the Pole, Ootah the Eskimo, not impressed by what they had done, remarked to Matthew Henson, "There is nothing here–just ice." But to the world's scientists, the explorers were standing not on barren ice, but on a certain point on the globe–the top of the world.

Chronology

1856 Robert E. Peary is born May 6 in Cresson, Pennsylvania.

1884 As a government engineer, Peary is sent to Central America to help find a path for an Atlantic-Pacific canal.

1886 Peary and Christian Maigaard explore Greenland; it is his first adventure in the far north.

1888 Marries Josephine Diebitsch.

1891 Backed by scientific societies, Peary takes leave from the navy and sets out to explore northern Greenland.

1893 Peary's wife Josephine gives birth to their daughter Marie on September 12, during an Arctic expedition.

1898 Peary begins a four-year probe into the Arctic, eventually failing in his quest to reach the North Pole.

1905 With a specially built ship, the *Roosevelt*, Peary renews his polar quest in July.

1906 Peary returns to New York in December after coming within 174 miles of the North Pole.

1908 On July 6, Peary leaves New York aboard the *Roosevelt* on his last expedition.

1909 Peary, Matthew Henson, and four Eskimos reach the North Pole on April 6.

1920 Robert Peary dies on February 20.

1990 The Navigation Foundation confirms that Peary truly reached the "near vicinity" of the North Pole as he claimed.

Arctic Circle–the ring of latitude around the earth located at 66 degrees north of the equator. Above it is the Arctic Ocean and polar ice pack.

aurora borealis–streaks of light that create wavy, throbbing patterns in the Arctic skies; also called "northern lights."

cairn–a monument of natural stones.

crevasse–a crack in the ice pack, sometimes so deep that the bottom cannot be seen from the surface.

draftsman–a professional who draws building and engineering design plans.

dry goods–nonfood supplies such as clothing.

floe–a vast sheet of floating ice in the Arctic Ocean.

gangrene–a dangerous condition that occurs when blood stops flowing to an injured area and the flesh begins to rot.

ice cap–the thick ice covering of the Arctic Ocean.

igloo–a hut made of ice blocks, used for housing and storage.

lead–an opening in the ocean surface between ice floes.

monolith–a massive, tall rectangular stone or structure.

Northwest Passage–a sea route between the Atlantic and Pacific Oceans that passes above North America along the polar ice cap.

pemmican–a compressed meat mixture favored by polar travelers because of its light weight and nourishment.

sledge–a heavy-duty sled, or platform on runners, used for hauling supplies over the Arctic and Antarctic ice.

tiller–a lever used to steer a boat from side to side.

Further Reading

Anderson, Madelyn Klein. *Robert E. Peary and the Fight for the North Pole*. New York: Franklin Watts, 1992.

Bartlett, Robert A. *The Log of Bob Bartlett*. New York: G.P. Putnam's Sons, 1928.

Charleston, Gordon. *Peary Reaches the North Pole*. New York: Dillon Press, 1993.

Davies, Thomas D. "New Evidence Places Peary at the Pole." *National Geographic* 100, no. 1 (January 1990): 44.

Dwyer, Christopher. *Robert Peary and the Quest for the North Pole*. Philadelphia: Chelsea House Publishers, 1992.

Gilman, Michael. *Matthew Henson*. Philadelphia: Chelsea House Publishers, 1988.

Herbert, Wally. *The Noose of Laurels*. New York: Atheneum, 1989.

Mountfield, David. *A History of Polar Exploration*. New York: Dial Press, 1974.

Owen, Russell. *The Conquest of the North and South Poles*. New York: Random House, 1952.

Schlesinger, Arthur M. jr., and Fred L. Israel, editors. *Robert E. Peary and the Rush to the North Pole: Chronicles from National Geographic*. Philadelphia: Chelsea House, 1999.

Picture Credits

DANIEL E. HARMON is associate editor of *Sandlapper: The Magazine of South Carolina* and editor of *The Lawyer's PC*, a national computer newsletter. He has written more than 20 nonfiction books on history, humor, and other topics. Harmon lives in Spartanburg, South Carolina.